44

D0896097

The best time is at night, in windy rain, an old oak groaning and creaking overhead. Naked and shivering, you stare at the steaming pool and put one foot in. The stinging tells you it's being cooked, yet other people are in up to their chins, laughing and beckoning. The cold rain encourages you in the cauldron. A searing line slowly rises to your chin and you don't dare move. Then, within five minutes, you feel melted and

happy, even into your bones. Someone passes a glass of wine. Pelted by rain it bubbles like champagne. Fifteen minutes later you rise into the wind—it feels delicious. Now you understand how the Finns can run naked from a sauna to hurl themselves into the snow. You sink easily back into the water again and gaze at the nude people, some standing in halos of steam, others hunched down to their chins. They all appear curiously pleased with themselves, & you think—what bliss!

HOT TUBS

How to Build, Maintain & Enjoy Your Own

by LEON ELDER

Photography by Sam Dabney,
Tim Crawford, Wayne McCall

Cartoons by Bruce MacDougall

CAPRA PRESS   1973   SANTA BARBARA

Copyright © 1973 by Capra Press

All rights reserved.

GRATEFUL ACKNOWLEDGMENTS TO: Walker A. Tompkins, Santa Barbara News-Press Historian for permission to reprint his article *"Hot Springs, 1888"*; Richard Johnston for permission to reproduce his *"Physical/Emotional Satisfaction Scale"* on page 53; Bruce MacDougall for his various cartoons; Graham Mackintosh for his diagram on page 22; Frank Frost for his construction diagrams on pages 58 & 59; George Christians for author's photo on page 79; Gretel Ehrlich for the coil photo on page 28; Margaret Dunlap for her sketch on page 19; Hokusai (18th cent.) for his print on page 12; Don Lothe for his graph help; and to the enthusiasm of Hot Tub owners, builders and soakers such as Fred Carr, Eric Cassirer, Patty Bruce, Lynn & Wendy Forman, Heidi, the Knolls, the Sanders, the Peakes, the Johnstons, the Dabneys, the Palmers, Pat McGinnis, Richard Petersen, John Smith, the McCalls, the de Milles, Tim Crawford, Vic Kondra, the Don Timms, Dr Lawrence Williams, Psychiatrist H. Neil Karp, Kerry and Tony Tomlinson, Linda Harwood, Kathy Koury, Judy & Molly Young, and others too coy to be mentioned.

ISBN 0-912264-57-8

CAPRA PRESS
631 State Street
Santa Barbara, Ca. 93101

Dedicated to warmth, trust & comraderie
in an overcrowded & suspicious world.

CONTENTS

HOT SPRINGS, 1888

By Walker A. Tompkins
News-Press Historian

When Wilbur Curtiss came to Santa Barbara in 1854 he was suffering from an incurable disease which doctors told him would end his life within six months. (Why doctors always granted a doomed patient six months more of life is as much a mystery as finding a cure for the common cold.)

Mr. Curtiss accepted his prognosis philosophically, but was determined to see as much of Santa Barbara's scenic wonders as time and strength permitted. Thus, during the course of a hike in the Montecito foothills, he encountered an old Indian bathing in Hot Springs Creek.

An Indian youth who accompanied Curtiss on his walks around the countryside indicated that this husky oldster was past his 110th birthday, and that he attributed his longevity to bathing in some hot springs which gushed from the cliffs farther up canyon

Wilbur Curtiss was curious to

9

see these health giving springs. A few hours' climb up the creek brought him to Montecito Hot Springs, which had been a popular bathing spa for soldiers of the Stevenson Regiment when they occupied Mexican Santa Barbara in 1847-48.

There were four springs, heated to 116 degrees, containing sulphur, arsenic, iron, magnesium and other health giving minerals.

Not having anything better to do, Curtiss soaked himself in the warm waters. He even drank from one of the sulphur springs. And a miracle happened: His health began to improve.

Six years later, when he obtained a homestead in Hot Springs Canyon which included the spa, Curtiss was a picture of vibrant health, and indeed lived to a ripe old age.

The fame of Curtiss' springs spread afar, and by the 1880s when Santa Barbara became a popular watering place for elite health seekers who had previously given their patronage to Baden-Baden, Spa, Aix-la-Chapelle or the thermal springs in Italy, the Montecito Hot Springs were a very valuable status symbol indeed.

In the late 1880s a three-galleried wooden hotel was built on a bench above the springs, as shown in the above rare picture from the past, reproduced from a stereoscope slide of 1888

Curtiss' homestead became the property of a stock company composed of wealthy individuals who furnished the Hot Springs Hotel with priceless antiques, oriental rugs and objects d'art. Mrs. Martin Kimberley, widow of the noted sea captain, and cofounder of Trinity Episcopal Church in 1869, was hired to operate the resort, which was open only to the upper crust of society.

After the turn of the century, the Hot Springs Hotel became even more exclusive; anyone with a bank account under seven digits need not apply.

In 1920 a disastrous forest fire cleaned out Montecito Hot Springs Canyon and leveled the hotel. It was rebuilt in 1923 under the ownership of a corporation limited to 17 members, all Montecito estate owners, who also controlled the Montecito Water Co.

H. B. Jones was the resident custodian of the new Hot Springs Hotel until it, too was destroyed in the Coyote Fire of 1964 It was his job to have baths ready for patrons who would telephone in advance of their arrival by limousine.

Today, a mile and a quarter hike up a dirt road from the end of Hot Springs Road brings one to the site of the old luxury spa. The mineral springs still flow as they did when the aborigines partook of their curative waters. There is even talk that a third, and hopefully fireproof, hotel will rise someday on the sandstone foundations of the old.

Foreword

THE PLEASURE of hot water soaking is universal and must go back to the Beginning. Cavemen, before the invention of fire, lounged in natural sulfur pools; Egyptians, Babylonians and Romans built tiled tubs. The spas of Europe gained early fame as Japan created its *furo* and Finland its *sauna*. Hawaiians, Turks, Abyssinians — peoples everywhere developed their own versions of thermal therapy. But it took contemporary California to make it fully social, where people were brought together unabashed in mixed company, as they say, sharing the bliss of the homemade, outdoor Hot Tub.

Yet who can legitimately lay claim to a universal invention? Do we credit an early man named Kyburz for inventing hot water, as Dick Johnston does, and then the Mountain Drivers for contriving the original Hot Tub; or do we recognize the possibility that when the cultural climate is fertile, an idea can generate simultaneously in many places?

It little matters. The Hot Tub, as described herein, is an established reality, though its true origin may be clouded. What follows now is a somewhat legendary account that grew from the hills of modest Santa Barbara where a recent census gives a Hot Tub count of forty-three, with five more under construction. If it suffers from provincialism, know too that it's true.

THE FIRST Hot Tub was observed in its native habitat in the foothills behind Santa Barbara on the night of the vernal equinox, back in nineteen aught and fifty-eight. It was a fine redwood tub steaming in the rain at the bottom of Will Henry's land, a short stroll down a dirt path from his adobe house. In the early evening the Tub stood unnoticed. Sounds of merriment, the music of recorder, concertina and pump organ, leaked from the windows during lulls in the lashing storm. The Mountain Drivers were having a banquet. An observer would have seen them in their most outlandish finery—gowns of theatre-curtain velvet, old graduation formals, Victorian dresses, and sequined shimmies from the twenties. One man in tails with a bemedaled sash across his chest, might have been a Bulgarian count. Another wore a wine-stained scoutmaster uniform. Next to him sat a crony in a canvas safari suit with a pith helmet that must have been nailed to his head—it never came off. Bobby Hyde, father-founder of this post-war community, lounged in his GI camouflage jumpsuit.

A book should be written about the Mountain Drivers, the phenomenon that they were. Call them a disparate group of young settlers who had no common ground except land. Or think of them as utopians struggling together for freedom and self-expression. It began at the end of WWII when Bobby Hyde, a visionary approaching fifty who had spent a quarter century building stone houses, writing books and playing Go, bought a hundred acres of steep, chaparral land behind Santa Barbara. A dirt road, called Mountain Drive, bisected this land. Bobby built his house on a prime saddle that looked down over the city to the harbor and the channel islands beyond. He planted olives and avocados around his house and encouraged young couples to build on his land. He sold it by the acre, fifty dollars down and fifty a month. This made it possible for most of them to have enough money left over to buy cement, nails, window glass and pipe. He let them use his cement mixer and gave them instruction on building walls, whether they be rammed earth, adobe or stone. He showed them the usefulness of old materials—railroad ties, telephone poles and freight car stakes, all virtually free in those days. He also showed them how to relax after a day's labor by loading them into his weapons carrier and driving them to the Las Cruces hot springs, in the hills forty miles away.

Most of these early Mountain Drivers were artists, wrtiers and craftsmen. One, however, was a mechanic and salesman who specialized in fifty-dollar cars and kept them running. Another was a specialist in old washing machines and water heaters.

Know that they were not harmoniously communal. They had no common belief, no credo, no organization. Many weren't even on speaking terms. But in spite of themselves they *were*, in the eyes of outsiders, a Group. As a group they either originated or perpetuated a number of ideas and institutions: the Mid-Summer's play and frolic, the Bobby Burns haggis banquet, the Grape Stomp, the Twelfth Night celebration, the philosophical Sunset Club, annual Pot Wars, and their mimeo paper, *The Grapevine*. They invented the car-stake module from those seven-foot timbers, using them for rafters and posts. They painted the word *WHOA* on county stopsigns marking boundaries to their domain

Many of their inventions and rituals had meaning only to them. But the one notable product of their ingenuity, one that spread like a small contagion beyond their world to be accepted enthusiastically elsewhere, was the home-made Hot Tub.

Henry and friends used much ingenuity to make that first Hot Tub hot. They contrived a makeshift system with diesel oil dripping into stove pipe with a vacuum cleaner turned backwards for a blower. They stacked fire brick for a heating chamber around cooiled copper tubing. It worked. The tub itself was the same redwood vat they used every year for the Grape Stomp and from which thousands of gallons of Kinevan Red had been bottled. Strange that, for all their inventiveness, the Mountain Drivers had never before conceived of using as a Hot Tub. They thought nothing of piling into Bobby's weapons carrier and driving two hours over mountain roads for a soak in Big Caliente or Las Cruces. There seemed no alternative.

Sheer torture it had always been, following a long hot soak, with your body soft and complacent, every nerve at peace begging for sleep, to dress and take a long jouncing ride home. Now with the backyard Hot Tub that ordeal was eliminated. In the years to come, as hot tubs began to proliferate, a prime principle was to place the tub as close to the bedroom as possible. After a soak the body craves bed.

Because of the weather that historic night, after the last lamb shank was licked clean, the Mountain Drivers stood and shed their garb around the table, using the chairs as clothes racks. The overdressed became undressed. Ladies with back zippers were obliged by the nearest gentleman. After a few minutes of contorting, everyone became his original self. "Welcome back, everybody!" exclaimed Peggy, shedding her Victorian dress. She plucked the tiara from her coifed hair, yanked out some strategic pins and let her hair tumble down over her bare shoulders. Will put on Handel's "Water Music". With that they scampered out into the rain, down the short path to where the Hot Tub awaited them.

One by one they lowered themselves in, ah, so gingerly. Soon enough they became comfortable, their heads in a ring resting against the redwood planks. They raised their glasses and toasted the "miraculous waters".

"Back in Baden-Baden," the erstwhile Bulgarian count began, "I bathed with cripples. The curative powers of that water were remarkable. One old geezer had to be wheeled

17

to the bath and lifted in. Yet, after an hour's soak, he literally danced away under his own power. In my notes at home, I think I have an analysis of that water. Now if we could just import dehydrated packets. . ."

"It's *all* right here!" cried Peggy. She climbed out of the tub, pranced over to a verdant bank and snatched up the spring's first canyon sunflowers and some springs of mint. By throwing them into the water, she became the first person to use additives in a Mountain Drive Hot Tub. "All ye of crippled humor and insomnia are hereby cured," she declared.

Whether they knew it then or not, a new life dimension was in the making. Bobby, the visionary, suggested rustling up more tubs and spotting them all over town so no one would ever be more than a mile away from one.

"Yep, hot tubs are here to say," mused Will Henry.

Some years later he inaugurated his Hot Tub Catering Service for the underprivileged. On the back of his dilapidated truck "Lupita", a Chevy one-tonner he brought back from Ensenada, he carried a redwood tub and a butane heating system.

A great number and variety of Hot Tubs began appearing both inside and outside the native habitat of Mountain Drive. While most of them are converted wine vats or water tanks, some are of concrete, mortared boulders and glassed plywood.

This book illustrates and desribes some of the working tubs in Santa Barbara. This does not include the commercial jacuzzis installed by swimming pool contractors. Nice as they are, they are expensive, "store-bought", and outside the scope of this book. We are dealing with the homemade Hot Tub, requiring only some ingenuity, romantic drive, work and a few dollars. The trick is in the resurrection and conversion of old parts by exploiting junk yards and cannibalizing old appliances.

Hot Tubs bring peace. As Chaucer wrote, *"His herte bathid in a bath of blisse."*

—Leon Elder
February 1973

THE WOODEN TUB

THE MOST COMMON hot tubs are wooden tanks, four to six feet in diameter. Although new ones are available, most of those seen in the Santa Barbara area are old and have been transplanted from farms or wineries. They are usually redwood, although some oak and even pine tubs have been seen. A redwood tank, set up properly, will last a lifetime or two. The fact that it has already spent 50 years storing farm water or fermenting grape juice has done little to shorten its life expectancy. Its very history is appealing to tub owners who take care to display whatever legend may have been stenciled on the side: "No Fishing", "Fermenter Vat No. 2", "Capacity 480 Gals." Tubs are given a respect. In this day of baroque, paisley and spray gun art that camouflages so many VW buses and bedroom walls, the hot tub stands stately and unadorned. The only alterations that owners can bring themselves to make are sculptural. Since most tubs come too tall, they have to be cut down, either all the way around or with scalloped entries. With some you get the feeling of boarding a boat.

For those of you who are not used to dealing with cubic figures it might be surprising to learn that a five-foot tub filled with three and a half feet of water is holding 515 gallons while a six footer holds 742 gallons. If you have reason to be concerned about the amount of water you use or fuel for heating, this can be a consideration. Also note that while a five foot tub will accommodate eight snuggling people (with a heroic ninth in the middle), a six footer will hold thirteen. The weight factor, which shouldn't matter if you are set up outdoors on firm ground, is two tons for a five footer and three tons for the six footer.

FINDING A TUB: Scour the nearby countryside for the sight of an old water tank, usually on stilts, that seems abandoned. The farmer, if he no longer uses it, might let you have it for the taking. It's an eyesore to him. If you don't have a crane or enough helpers to move it bodily, get yourself a can of Liquid Wrench, a heavy crescent wrench and a bright crayon. Be sure to number all the staves in sequence before dismanteling. They are not all identical, are slightly beveled and some have been hewn to fit between their neighbors. In a sense, you are taking apart a handfitted boat. The floor planking too should be key-marked to show where they fit into grooves near the ends of the staves.

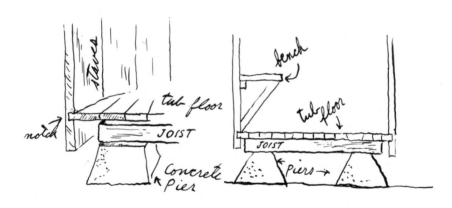

The hoops surely will be rusted. Several inches of thread will protrude through each nut. With liberal dosings of Liquid Wrench, a wrench and muscle, you should be able to persuade the hoops to open—like bracelets. It's a good idea to number the hoops as well and even to mark where on the thread the nut was cinched up to.

Reassembling the tank will be tricky. A few friends can help hold the staves while you slip on the hoops and take up the slack. Best if you scour all faces of each stave with a wire brush before assembling so that you get tight joints of clean wood.

If you find no water tank on a farm, try a winery. Many are converting from wood to stainless steel these days and might be willing to sell you an old fermenter. Check the smaller wineries. The big operators seem only to have tubs the size of rooms.

If nothing turns up at a farm or winery, you can build your own or buy a new one from a cooper. If you do elect to build a wooden tub it's advisable to stay with a square or rectangular shape. A round one takes special expertize. Only people with the tools and know-how of Fred Carr, builder of the automated oval tub, should undertake such a project.

For the record, mention should be made of prefab fiberglass tanks available in Hollywood, naturally. They cost more than wood and don't feel loving.

A good cooper and dealer in both new and used tanks is Alex McCollom of San Jose, California.

INSTALLATION: Clear a fairly level area as close to a bedroom as possible since a deep relaxed sleep is the natural aftermath of a good soak. Dig four one-foot holes at the corners of a square approximately six inches smaller than the diameter of your tub. In these set four concrete foundations piers which can be bought precast at lumber yards for about a dollar apiece. Level them in a generous puddle of concrete. These will support two joists, four by fours are sturdy enough. These can be easily leveled with shims. Best give them a slight slope, about one inch over five feet, toward the side the drain will be.

The ingenious Squire, who built the gazebo tub, installed a shock absorber under the edge of his tub opposite the drain. It automatically lifted the tub as it emptied, so the last inch of sediment drained out.

Set the tub directly on the joists at a right angle to the floor planks. It is very important that the joists are cut to fit *inside* the staves and support *only the floor of the tub*. These tanks are designed for the hoops to contain the water. The structure would be violated if the weight were taken by the stave ends. The groove that receives the bottom planking would twist or crack. These grooves usually need to be sealed. Fill them with a paste of chicken mash before they are tapped onto the floor planking. It worked wonders for Fred Carr, builder of the oval tub.

Don't screw or bolt the tub to the joists. It won't go anywhere.

Now that the tub is assembled, install your planks for seating about eighteen inches from the bottom. A pair of two by tens cut to conform to the curve are wide enough. Support with a leg near each end and attach with glued dowels or brass angle fittings. Be sure any screws or holes don't go all the way through the staves.

Your tub now, like a new wooden boat, won't hold water well. You've cinched up the hoops, everything looks tight. You fill it with a hose and to your horror, it sprouts a hundred leaks. Be patient. As the hours pass the wood will swell and the leaks will disappear. Rather than filling your tub immediately, a better plan is to put in a sprinkler and let it spray the wood for a few hours, even overnight. A good tub will swell and become watertight without caulking. But in the cases of some older tubs that have suffered the ravages of weather, weevils and woodpeckers, caulking may be necessary, particularly when you can see daylight through some joints. Boat shops have a good new plastic putty that can be applied to wet surfaces. Then too, as a final resort and if the tub seems too far gone even for caulking, you can glass it as they do surfboards, with resin and matt cloth. The only real objection is aesthetic. Most hot tub soakers don't like the feel of plastic and insist that wood is the only compatible material to lean against.

Once your tub is filled it should always have some water left in to keep it tight. A glassed tub, however, can be emptied and left dry.

Your next step is to drill two holes—a high inlet just below water level about 42 inches above the floor, and an outlet at the bottom. The best fitting to use is a bronze through-hull that boat chandleries carry. They come in different sizes. A three-quarter or one-inch size is recommended for most systems. They are expensive, however (approximately $5 ea.) and many tub owners have simply pounded rigid pipe through a tight hole which has been doped with silicone mastic. Even if a slight leak develops it will just provide a humid environment for any mint or ferns you might plan around the base of the tub.

The tub now needs a cover or lid, something light and easily removable that will keep out leaves and dirt and which will hold in the heat. For its insulation, wood is favored, even something as thin as quarter-inch ply-wood reinforced by a couple of 1x2 ribs to prevent warping. Another suggestion is a canvas tonneau that snaps around the edges. Keep your tub covered when not in use as safety for children as well as small wild creatures such as lizards, mice and frogs.

So now there she sits, the noble tub, tight with water and waiting to be heated.

IS IT WORTH IT?

HEATERS: You have, say, 500 gallons of cool water and you now must bring it up to at least 105^0. Since there's no practical way of doing this in one pass (the average household heater holds merely 30 gallons), you must recirculate the water through a heating system many times to make it hot. If you begin with 60^0 degree water, it will take from two to sixteen hours, depending upon the kind of heater you have scrounged up.

If gas is handy there are many cheap, even free, types of heaters available. The most common, though the least efficient, is the familiar household tank heater. Junkyards are full of them. Often there is no more wrong than a small leak and you can often get one for the asking. You are operating a low-pressure system, and many won't leak at all with your hookup. Set your heater so the top is fairly close to the water level of the tub. Take a line from the drain outlet of your tub (here it's a good idea to put in a tee with a hose bib facing straight out so you can irrigate your trees or garden with used tub water) to the bottom drain nipple of the heater. Cap off the cold water pipe on top of the heater, then run a line from the hot water side to the tub's inlet. This simple plumbing can be done with galvanized, copper, schedule 40 plastic pipe or heavy duty appliance hose as in washing machines. Plastic pipe is the cheapest, the easiest to work with and has good insulation. It will cut down heat loss many times over metal pipe. Its only drawback is its tendency to sag and should be supported in spans over two feet.

If it's a tank heater you must have, remember that a small 20-galloner will heat as quickly as a larger one and be less conspicuous. Still, your circulating water will only be heating at two or three degrees an hour.

A much better heater is the coil type enclosed in a cast iron casing. Fifty years ago these household "side-arm" heaters were common. A gas burner on the bottom heats coiled copper tubing and is twice as efficient as the tank heater. Watch the junkyards for these. They show up sometimes from old demolished houses. They will heat your water four or five degrees an hour.

For super fast heating, 25 degrees an hour, snoop for a "flash" heater such as a Ruud Model 100. They are used by laundromats, car washes, hotels, and many institutions. You'll need a bigger gas line, one inch instead of half inch, and they roar when they're fired up. To heat a thousand gallons of water in an hour or so is spectacular. It allows you to be spontaneous and have almost an instant hot tub soak if the right people unexpectedly show up on the horizon. If one of these doesn't appear in a junkyard, check with your local swimming pool equipment company.

If natural gas isn't available, you can use portable butane tanks. Then there are kerosene, oil, and electric heaters, although the latter is usually ruled out for expense. The army developed an immersible kerosene heater that kept garbage cans of dishwater piping hot. Though we've never seen one in a Hot Tub, it's conceivable it would do the job. But the fumes wouldn't be pleasant and it would have to be removed to make room for people. As a last resort, build a wood or coal fire directly under a system of copper coils.

Several Santa Barbara tubs use solar heating as a supplement. It won't get the water hot enough by itself, but it will help to maintain the temperature on sunny days. The system is to snake fifty feet of half-inch copper tubing painted black over a reflective underlay on a rooftop. Black hose is almost as good. We have heard of sophisticated solar heating systems that use sealed glass absorbers that can boil water, but this is beyond the technology of this book.

P U M P S : Since the water must be kept circulating through the system, a pump is necessary. Simple convection will work, but slowly, and is susceptible to vapor lock if the water is heated too fast. You don't really need much of a pump unless you have a big flash heater or install a filter. You need only enough pump to keep the heating water moving. There is nothing to gain by circulating vast amounts of water through a relatively slow heater. Look for old washing machine pumps, bilge pumps, booster pumps, swimming pool or garden fountain pumps. Most types have built-in motors, some are submergible, others require a small external motor. In any case, ground the line from the pump and motor back to the house ground. Sears sells a Ground Fault Circuit Interrupter which gives protection from electrical leaks too small to trip a circuit breaker, but strong enough to be dangerous.

The pump should be mounted low, between the tub outlet and the heater so it will keep its prime. It should be accessible for periodic cleaning and oiling and best be shielded from the weather by a box. Some pumps are noisy. This can be reduced by mounting it on a rubber pad and using rubber hose connections to the pipe.

Be sure to screen the outlet hole inside the tub to keep foreign matter, such as berries, leaves and jewelry, out of the system. Use copper, aluminum or brass screen, of course.

Always turn the pump on before lighting the heater, otherwise you could be faced with a steamy blow-out a while later. Keep those hundreds of gallons of water nicely flowing when the heater is on. When the water is not hot enough, turn the heater down or off. At night when the lid is off and people in, the tub water temperature will drop rather quickly unless you keep the burners at simmer. (Continued on page 49)

A Gallery of Hot Tubs

POSTED
NO
FISHING

(Continued from page 32)

FILTERS: Most Mountain Drive tubs are without filters, though that means changing the water every day or two. Since most of the owners have thirsty orchards or vegetable crops, it's no concern. The installation of a good filter means that you should rarely need to change water. But it is another expense and something else to take care of. Swimming pool contractors and supply houses seem to be the best source of filters. A common type is a diatomaceous earth disc filter rated for 10,000 gallon capacity. Circulate water through the filter at least two hours a day and flush out filter bags every week. There is also a paper cone filter system. Pump and filter come in a single unit, selling new for about $20. The cone filter units, however, are fairly expensive and need replacement about twice a month.

If you do install a filter, you might as well add an automatic timer and a thermostat that uses 24 volts from a step-down transformer. That will give you a deluxe hot tub system offering you a good soak at any hour, day or night. A dial setting and it's done. This is optional, of course. Most Mountain Drive tubs aren't used more than every week or so. The hot tub soak is considered an Event. The scrubbing, filling and actual lighting of the heater is a toastworthy occasion.

49

ADDITIVES: Since used wine tanks are usually very acid, neutralize your first tubful of water with soda ash. For approximately four dollars you can buy a PH kit. It is desirable to maintain the PH at 7 to 7.4 to give the most life to chlorine. Michael Peake recommends pouring five or six glugs of liquid chlorine around the water's perimeter each day. Then too, it's good to "shock" the tank every six weeks with a half gallon of chlorine if you have a filter system. Add swimming pool acid (cyanic acid) if the water becomes too alkaline.

The faint chlorine smell is unfortunate, but can be disguised in many ways. This can be left to your own invention, but noteworthy additives that followed Peggy's bouquet of mint, have been jasmine blossoms, oil of winter green, sassafras, essence of orange, sage, patchouli oil and any of the spa mineral salts on the market. The latter smell authentic, if not good. Anyone laved with suntan oil should be asked to shower first. It is highly polluting.

For diversion, Mountain Drivers have, on occasion, added floating balloons, flotillas of wind-up toy boats, rubber ducks, bubble bath, floating candles and even a portable underwater bubble hose that gave everyone the jollies one zany moonlit night.

LIGHTING: This subject confronts us with delicately differing Schools of Thought. One calls for the very dimmest of lighting, presumably because there are features best hidden, or that in darkness there is more freedom to cuddle. The other School wants ample light so to admire the vision of their happy nude friends. It seems best to have your lighting flexible to suit the temper of the soakers. In any case, lighting should be soft, as produced by candles and lanterns. One of the more festive tub scenes is lit by Christmas tree lights strung in an overhead tree. Many tub sessions are in daylight, illuminated by the smiling sun.

51

TEMPERATURE: This is a matter of dispute, controversy and personal tolerance. People's thresholds vary greatly. A delicate newcomer may withdraw a timorous foot from 104^0 water exclaiming, "Ouuu, it's *scalding!*" A seasoned Japanese *furo* soaker will find anything under 120^0 cool. We find the most congenial temperature for westerners is 106^0. At that point you can soak comfortably for an hour, occasionally sitting up on the edge for a cool airing, and receive the full benefits of thermal relaxation. But if you want the heat to penetrate your bones, try $110\text{-}112^0$. You won't stay in as long, but it brings deeper satisfaction. As a rule then, 106^0 is best for socializing, while 110^0 is most therapeutic. Buy a good underwater thermometer and use it. A few degrees makes a great difference. At least two Hot Tub owners have their thermometers wired to elec tronic dials mounted indoors so they can keep a close eye on temperature.

One of the most experienced Hot Tub owners, Dick Johnston, having observed a correlation between temperature and the behavior of his guests over the years, became inspired to research the phenomenon. He embraced the findings of Kyburz (ca. 1200 B.C.), inventor of hot water, added his own observations and devised *"The Johnston-Kyburz Physical/Emotional Satisfaction Scale"* which he consented to have reproduced on the next page:

52

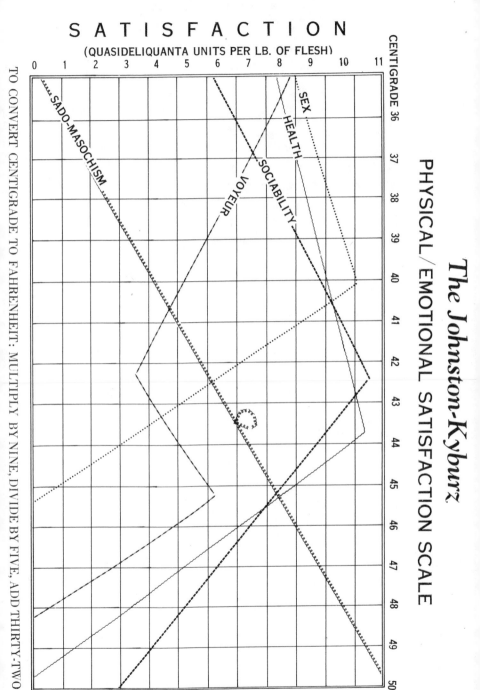

The Johnston-Kyburz

PHYSICAL/EMOTIONAL SATISFACTION SCALE

SATISFACTION

(QUASIDELIQUANTA UNITS PER LB. OF FLESH)

0 1 2 3 4 5 6 7 8 9 10 11

CENTIGRADE 36 37 38 39 40 41 42 43 44 45 46 47 48 49 50

SADO-MASOCHISM

VOYEUR

SOCIABILITY

HEALTH

SEX

TO CONVERT CENTIGRADE TO FAHRENHEIT: MULTIPLY BY NINE, DIVIDE BY FIVE, ADD THIRTY-TWO

AMENiTiES: Provide pegs for towels and clothes near the tub, a bench or log to sit on while removing footgear, a hammock or two to dream in after a soak, and a ring of narrow shelves around the tub for wine cups. Most tub owners forbid glass in the tub area and furnish plastic or paper cups. Broken glass underwater is nearly impossible to see. In parts of Hawaii, where Hot Tubs are known, a small one-man barrel of cold water adjoins the communal tub. From time to time a soaker douses his pinkened body in it, and emerges exhilirated. Similarly, a cold water hose nearby will accomplish much the same thing. Claims are made that hot-cold alterations are great for skin tone.

It's pleasant to enclose the tub area in arbors and trellises. Flowering vines, such as honeysuckle, jasmine and cirius will ingratiate the air. Consider too, installing a small speaker to a nearby tree or wall.

HEALTH: Physicians confirm what we already know—hot tub soaking is beneficial. It relaxes muscles, dilates blood vessels and helps circulation. Buoyancy helps venous return. It is good for people with heart trouble, varicose veins and high blood pressure. Older people who have suffered previous strokes, however, should be cautioned against soaking alone. Those with hardening of the arteries should abstain. Contrary to common belief, a hot bath does not help to dissipate a fever and should then be avoided. Nor is it a cure of intoxication. Otherwise, a Hot Tub soak is heartily recommended.

PSYCHIATRIC ASPECTS: Psychiatric authorities, such as Rollo May, have characterized our era as schizoid, in which we are thrown together in an increasingly crowded world yet feel a growing sense of isolation and estrangement. People crave closeness, yet find themselves unable to achieve it.

Various people have sought solutions, one of which is communal living. Another is a growing movement—the communal hot tub as discussed in this book. This offers a solution and an attempt to provide the closeness which everyone craves. By its very nature—a small group soaking together nude in a heated tub—a sense of warmth and community is provided.

The small hot tub might be considered a womb-like milieu especially conducive to relaxation and openness. The nudity might well express an attitude which could be an antidote to the often frustrating attempts to achieve intimacy through mechanical sexuality. It could also promote a healthy atmosphere in which one could overcome shyness or oversensitivity about body image or fear of exposure.

In summary, I believe the communal hot tub represents a very sane approach towards overcoming the schizoid trends in our society by providing a relaxed and meaningful intimacy.

—H. Neil Karp, M.D.
psychiatry

OTHER TYPES OF TUBS

THE CANNIBAL POT: The simplest, and in some ways the best, answer to the mechanics in hot tubbery was conceived and built by Frank Frost.   It resembles a giant concrete soup bowl, stuccoed on the outside and ringed by inlaid tile.   In the bottom he inserted a thick iron plate which conducts heat from a simple gas burner that slides underneath.   The water is heated directly, with no need for pumps, plumbing or elaborate heaters.   When the water reaches the desired temperature Frost, like an alert chef, simply turns off the gas.   His guests call it the cannibal pot, but only become apprehensive when he appears at tubside with onions and carrots.   Here are his construction diagrams:

1.

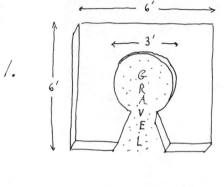

Make a concrete foundation 4" high. Dig out the middle a foot deep and fill with gravel. This is for drainage during rain or overflows.

2.

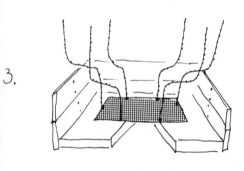

get a ¼" steel plate 3+ feet sq. weld reinforcing rods to it as shown after bending rods into shape. (your ironmonger will weld for you.)

3.

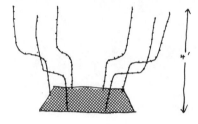

put the plate over the "keyhole". build forms out of old 2 x 10's. You are going to have concrete poured to cover the horizontal bend in the rods.

4.

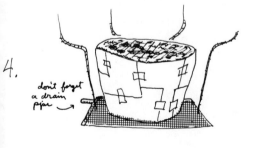

don't forget a drain pipe →

to form up the center depression take cardboard cartons, cut them up and tape them to make a cylinder. then fill the cylinder with tightly packed dirt. the concrete man will giggle, but it works.

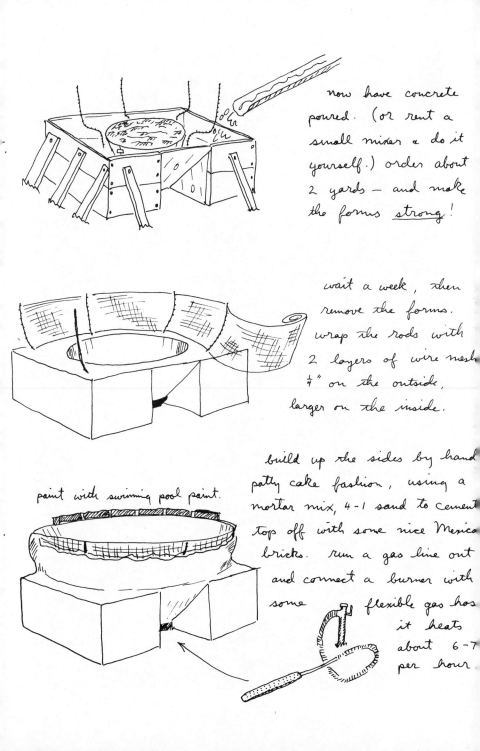

now have concrete poured. (or rent a small mixer & do it yourself.) order about 2 yards — and make the forms **strong**!

wait a week, then remove the forms. wrap the rods with 2 layers of wire mesh $\frac{1}{4}$" on the outside, larger on the inside.

build up the sides by hand patty cake fashion, using a mortar mix, 4-1 sand to cement top off with some nice Mexican bricks. run a gas line out and connect a burner with some flexible gas hose it heats about 6-7 per hour.

paint with swimming pool paint.

THE GREENHOUSE POOL: In the oaks behind their stone house, Jon and Zig Knoll had a sturdy old glass greenhouse, long neglected. Their interest was in growing edible things like avocados, oranges, apricots and vegetables, making exotic wines, raising worms and grinding compost. Zig is also a belly dancer and poet, Jon a research engineer. They had a mutual need to soak away the tensions of their busy lives, and had no interest in raising orchids. So one fine day, with sledge and pick, they attacked the concrete greenhouse floor and bashed through a five foot circle. Then they dug. A few weekends later they had themselves a sunken hot pool of reinforced concrete and a neat system of pipes and valves, perfectly planned and executed. A fountain pump circulates water between a 20-gallon tank heater and the pool or, by a turning of valves, pumps it out into their orchard through a hose. The pool provides an ideal climate for a huge, looming staghorn fern and friends in need.

THE BOULDERED POOL: The most idyllic tub, where man's handiwork is nearly invisible, is John Smith's bouldered pool. The bottom of his land extends through an oak grove, an ancient waterway where room-sized boulders were casually tossed. Here, on a narrow plateau that parallels the presentday creek, Smith found a perfect nest of boulders. He excavated a few yards of leaf mold, hit buried boulders and mortared the seams, troweling in a fairly smooth bottom. When filled with hot water no one would suspect that it wasn't a natural hot spring. Since it is a great distance from a gas line, he must lug in a couple of portable butane tanks to fuel his heater which stands like a sentry alongside the pool. The only real drawback to a bouldered tub is that the stones soak up much heat in the beginning. But once they have done their absorbing, they tend to keep the water warm. To take the trail down through a sloping avocado orchard, winding through the oak grove, parting the final branches and to see revealed this steaming pool, is a visit to Eden.

THE PLYWOOD TUB: In striking contrast is the sunken plywood tub Vic Kondra found in the backyard of a house he just bought in a conventional neighborhood. It is surrounded by decking, fencing on two sides, and an arbor. The previous owner, Don Timm, had given a summer of ambition and energy to build his personal spa. He began by digging a rectangular hole six by eight feet, three feet deep. He lined it with three-quarter inch marine plywood which he glassed on both sides. He built in a pair of benches running the long way. One was 16 inches high for short people (their children), and the other was 12 inches high for grownups. His wife, with talents as a muralist, painted the inner walls with sweeping aquarian designs. Kondra likes his water hotter than any westerner we know—a piping 120^0. With a super "Aldheet" 420,-000 BTU flash heater, he heats a thousand gallons of cold water in less than an hour and a half.

THE CUDDLE TUB: Isla Vista, adjoining the UCSB campus, has a road called El Nido (The Nest) where there is a grove of tall Island pines. In one of them is a gigantic crow's nest which is actually a house where lives a boat-builder. At the foot of the tree is a fence corner and another kind of nest—a water nest. It is Richard Peterson's cuddle tub, barely 24 inches square and 27 inches high. Unbelievably, it holds two people—if they are compatible. It's a simple box made of two by tens, doweled, pegged, glued and then glassed with resin. A regular sink drain was installed in the bottom. Hot water is piped over from the water heater of a nearby house. "We even got a third nestled in here one night," Peterson said, "but don't ask me how."

THE YIN YANG POOLS: Carved into the cliffs above the ocean is a pair of interlocking spiraled pools on a tiled terrace below the house of Eric Cassirer. A three HP industrial pump pushing water through a four inch main at the rate of 400 gallons per minute gives the water motion and activates a series of two inch jet streams. The first is aimed at your feet and, as you follow the curve into deeper water, others play upon your knees, waist and shoulders. Cassirer designed and plumbed these hot pools after studying the spas of Europe. Adjoining the pools he built a cold cascading waterfall. Directly behind is a bath house with a sauna and a massage room.

The ocean, on this part of the coast, is to the south. The pools are oriented so that you can lie the shallows, your head to the north, and watch passing ships and whales. You are in the attitude of a compass needle, a clue to the further meaning that Cassirer gives his facility—*vitron energy awareness*. At the very edge of the cliff he had welded a steel tripod tower which he claims serves as an energy antenna. Its base encloses a tubful of magnetite sand over which hangs a magnet. This tower is tied in to the steel webbing embedded in the pools' concrete, and into the reinforcing rods of the stone walls. The stones themselves he trucked in from Mexico for their energy potential. All this is to implement his own massage techniques designed to draw energy up from the legs through body blocks and thus to sensitize the whole person.

It is inspiring enough to lie in this pool on the cliff on the edge of the western world, feel the sea breeze across your face and gaze at the breathing ocean.

AFTERWORD & FOREWARNING

IF YOU DO go ahead and build your own Hot Tub it's like adding a room to your life, if not a new dimension. You soon learn that while few bodies are classically beautiful, none are ugly. To compare the fat to the lithe is like juxtaposing a Lachaise to a Giacometti. You've soaked with infants, grandparents and all ages in between, and have learned there are neither terrible secrets nor mysteries of the universe to be seen. Secrets and mysteries are as elusive as ever, but you have gained a *quality* of comraderie that is unique.

Your life has expanded, but so have your chores. It's one thing to get the tub ready—the filling and heating, trimming the candles, folding up towels and laying a fire for the aprés bath—that's only half of it. The dirty work comes the morning after as you discover soggy footprints have tracked up your house, the empty beer cans and little hills of dirty towels, anonymous garments, and the murkiness of the tub itself. Whatever happened to that sparkling water that surged from the hose? You had forgotten to put the lid on at bedtime and now dead leaves are coasting on the surface. Some have become waterlogged and have sunk to join a maroon sock on the bottom. You reach for it and yelp—the water is a scalding 140^0 because you forgot to turn off the heater.

You groan as you remember last night's crisis. You had invited Bill and Mary Newcomer over, little suspecting they were having marital problems. At Hot Tub time

Mary had gaily stripped with the others and romped down to the tub. He preferred to fume and pace the house. Now and then he'd stomp out on the porch and yell down at the tub, "Big deal!" He refused to go in himself or give her reprieve. Ugly, but it happens sometimes making you, the host, feel somehow responsible, though you know you're not.

You screw a long hose onto the drain valve and pull it down the slope with you to the new trees. As the tub water fills the basin of a young avocado you think of the nourishment it's getting, more than plain water would give. You had eleven happy people over last night, and one grump. The grump didn't get in, so really what you are doing now is giving happy water to your tree.

Later, after you've given the tub its scrubdown and gaze at the new water filling it, you catch yourself humming with expectation. You turn on the pump and heater eagerly. It's then you realize you've become a tub freak.

MY FATHER GOT IT
SOMEWHERE — HE
USED TO BE A MISSIONARY..

ENCOURAGING WORDS

I first saw, and felt, a classical Japanese *furo* in Kokura while on R and R from the Korean War. The luxury of being enveloped by 110^0 water was matched only by the companionship; there was I, a timid American, huddled in my corner, while whole smiling Japanese families filed in and out of the huge communal vat, exclaiming with delight to one another as the molten liquid dissolved their sinews. At that time I vowed I would someday have my own party-sized tub, thinking that such an appliance would be unique in America.

It was only a few years later that I moved to Santa Barbara and found that there were indeed hot tubs in America and that most of them were in Santa Barbara. I had been in many of the town's tubs when, years later, it was finally possible for me to build my own, and I am no less pleasured by a tub and good fellowship now than I was my first time twenty-two years ago in Kokura.

So far as I know, Santa Barbara remains the hot tub capital of America, and as a public official of that part of Santa Barbara County where hot tubism was born, I invite readers of all origins, creeds, cults and karasses to investigate this aspect of our indigenous culture, to be inspired and to help spread this most civilized of customs through a deserving world.

—Supervisor Frank J. Frost

Soaking is not a body concert. Those who have tubs are not entertaining orgies. The familiarity of the tub is essential, not sexual. Being a belly dancer I easily testify to the healing power of the tub. Aches and pains disappear in the water. Two hours dancing to an hour's soaking. Our hot tub is a great fluid mother who soothes our anxieties while we warm in her belly.

—Zig Knoll

Having sat, floated, or floundered in countless hot tubs with friends of all sexes, I divine that women feel differently about bare groups than men do. It may go all the way back to the baboon or to the abominable screwman, but I think we must admit that men are sexually more aggressive than women are. Bare men don't admire each other much. Bare women may admire each other, or may pretend to if they feel bitchy . . . At any rate, all this discord and uptightness gets washed away by hot water. Sink into the tub, and you'll begin to shed the dead skin of your previous persona and find a smoother one underneath. It happens when you sit around with naked friends and neighbors for a few hours. Suddenly you realize you are looking at persons instead of bodies. The bareness just makes you feel that each person is easier to get to. This accessibility can be an illusion, of course. The man or woman who can't give out any tenderness or expose any vulnerability with clothes on probably can't learn to do it with clothes off either. But often it is real.

You have to start with people you can trust, people who respect you, people who can take you the way you are, people who find you trustworthy, respectful, and accepting, too. A tall order! But then you can find yourself facing a sweet, open soul, whose undefended body keeps whispering, "Here I am. Look at me. Take me. I'm yours. I'm not holding anything back." And you realize that you love that person. Next time you meet, you put your arms around each other and say, "Remember when we were in the womb together?" And he or she says, "Yes, yes," and squeezes you and sighs a big sigh, and it is hardly erotic at all, but it is lovely.

—Callista McAllister

Santa Barbara must be the world center for the Hot Tub as described in this book. Santa Barbara has almost a utopian climate; it never gets very cold or very hot, and evenings when hot-bathing is at its best are often blessed with warm gentle breezes coming off the Santa Ynez mountains, and these airs are laden with the scent of blooming pittosporum or jasmine, and if the flowers fail a drop of patchouli oil in the water is very nice.

Some say, "Solitary bathing is a sin." And truly, once one has experienced the languid delight, the magnificent sociability and the beauty of the invigorating aftermath of the outdoor hot tub, one tends to agree. A hot tub gathering shouldn't be considered as a lewd bacchanal. I prefer to think of a hot bath as a beautiful orgy *without* sex. I recommend it heartily. Solitary bathing *is* a sin.

—Dick Johnston

In far off lands and times gone by, each man knew his place and function. When to bow first, when second. Where to command, where to obey. Whom to touch, whom to shun. Everyone had his own village, tribe, or lodge, his own religion, caste, or class. The family bulged with grandparents, uncles, cousins, aunts and hangers-on. Each person was secure in his own group, understood by all according to his role.

Now we drift on a vast, heaving plane littered with campers and trailers, strewn with abandoned careers, suburban bedrooms, broken homes, planned slums, transferred employees, and fortified condominia. Everyone is our neighbor, but no one is our friend. Surviving grandparents have defected to retirement colonies. Childhood chums are scattered by the winds of opportunity. Our living quarters are too small, our schedules too tight, or our standards too strict to accommodate visiting clansmen. Hemmed in on all sides, we feel bereft and alone.

The hot tub temporarily shuts out this unsatisfying world and restores our sense of community. Bathed in its comforting warmth, we ritually re-enact our common origin. Instant amniotic comrades, we need no roles to play, but gaze contentedly into each other's faces, wondering where the boundary between one person and another lies, or if there is a boundary. Born again into the cold night air, we find ourselves once more discrete individuals, but no longer isolated, as the memory of that brief, unspoken coalescence lingers and glows.

—Richard de Mille

CRAWFORD by DABNEY   DABNEY by CRAWFORD

MACDOUGALL by MACDOUGALL   ELDER by CHRISTIANS

This book, designed by Noel Young for Capra Press, was set in linotype Trump Mediaeval by Graham Mackintosh, with Albertus, Gold Rush, Stencil and Trump Bold Italic for display, and was printed and bound by Stecher-Traung-Schmidt in San Francisco, April 1973.